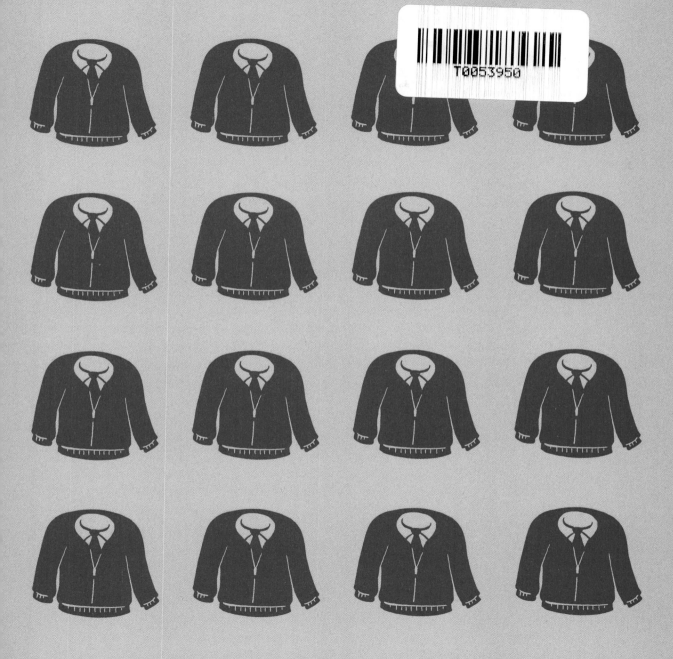

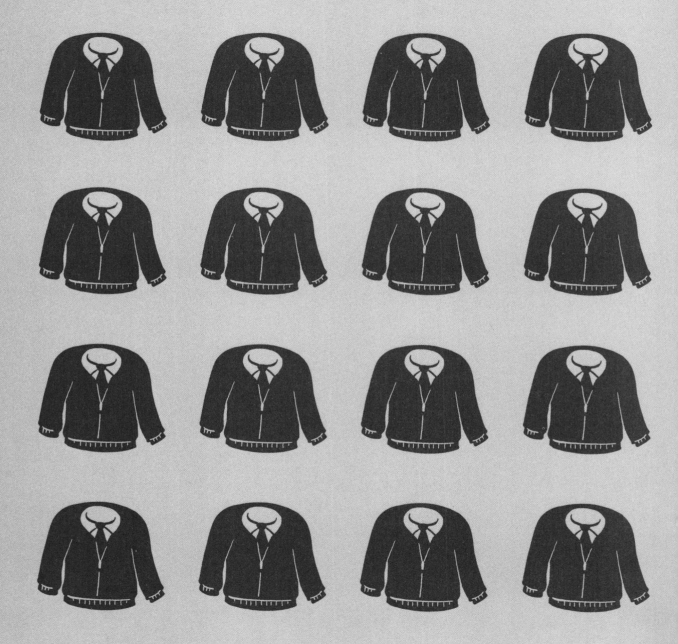

I am Mister Rogers

BRAD MELTZER

illustrated by Christopher Eliopoulos

ROCKY POND BOOKS

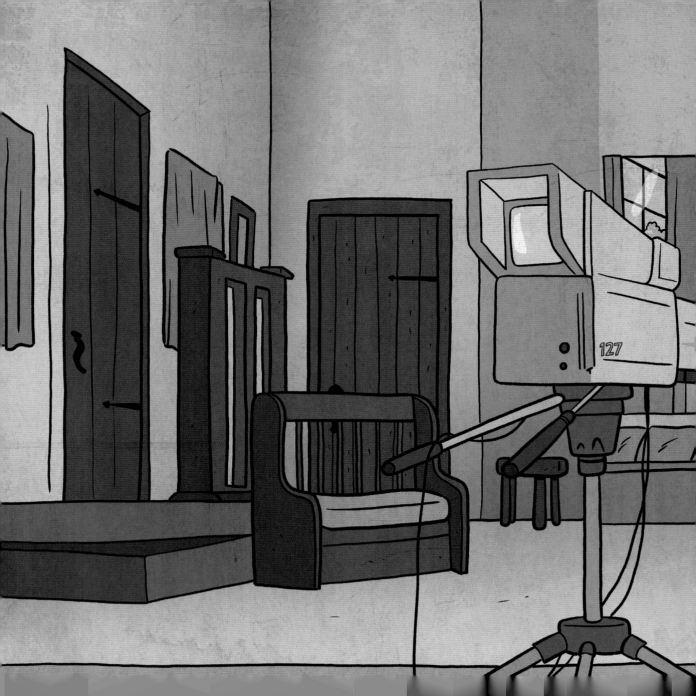

Hi, neighbor.

I am MISTER ROGERS.

I grew up in a town called Latrobe, Pennsylvania. It was a small town—with a real trolley—the kind of place where everyone knew their neighbors.

When I was little, I wasn't popular.
I was shy and didn't like sports.
Bullies would call me names.
One day, as I was walking home, I had the feeling
that I was being followed.

Sure enough, some boys were behind me.
I started walking faster... and they started walking faster, getting
closer and louder.

I was mad at those kids—and felt bad that they couldn't see me as anything but shy and weak.

I cried in my room.
A lot.

I was scared of many things, like going to the doctor...

being alone...

and starting school.

I DON'T WANT TO GO.

FREDDY, YOU HAVE TO.

I once ordered an exercise kit to give me big muscles. It didn't work.

But you see, there's nothing wrong with being scared.

It's all right to feel how you're feeling.

I was also sick a lot as a kid, with diseases like scarlet fever and asthma. Stuck in bed by myself, I'd use my toys and make up stories.

I'd pretend my knees were mountains.

I CAN MAKE IT TO THE SUMMIT!

Then the adventure would begin. I'd enter my world of make-believe.

ALMOST AT THE SUMMIT!

Eventually, I added puppets—and even had my own puppet theater in our attic. It had a real stage, where I'd entertain family and friends.

Telling those make-believe stories helped me feel so much better.

HE'S REALLY GOOD AT THIS.

143

Something else that helped me when I was worried or sad was music.

My dad and I would parade through the house, banging and strumming away on instruments.

Music is the one art we all have inside.

We may not be able to play an instrument, but we can all sing along or tap our feet.

I took the trolley by myself to downtown Pittsburgh.
For hours, I played every piano in the store.

The next day, the salesperson couldn't believe it when I came back with a check from my grandmother.

Finally...

THIS IS THE ONE.

≤AHEM≥ ARE YOU SURE YOU CAN AFFORD IT?

It was a secondhand 1920 Steinway.

MY NANA SAYS HI.

That piano changed my life, giving me confidence and comfort.
But it wasn't just a piano that my grandmother gave me.
It was love.

It was the same with my grandfather Fred McFeely, whom I was named after.
He'd teach me about the world and myself.
And after each visit, he'd say to me...

He helped me realize how valuable every human being is, including myself.
Isn't that beautiful?

The love from a grandparent is so special.

Love is at the root of everything: all learning, and teaching, and relationships.

My parents, especially my mom, taught me the value of sharing that love with others. When she heard that a student couldn't afford new shoes, she bought him brand-new high-tops.

Over time, the school nurse would order coats, eyeglasses, even furniture, and send the bills to my mom, who never took credit.

Wouldn't it be great if love like that was shown to all kids?

Every Christmas, she'd make new sweaters for everyone in our family.

She had all these different patterns.

When I would see scary things in the news as a boy, my mother would repeat one of my life's great lessons...

My senior year of high school, I saw
something that changed my life:
Television.

WHOA.

The show I was watching had people throwing pies at each other.

ISN'T IT
GREAT?

I'M NOT
SURE ABOUT
THAT.

I couldn't understand why this new device was being used to make fun
of people when it could instead be such a wonderful tool for education.
But there was one thing I knew for sure:
I wanted to work in television.

My first job was in New York at NBC.
One of the stars of the show used to talk directly to the camera.

I asked him how he connected to his audience when they weren't in the studio and he couldn't see them.

My real break came when a Pittsburgh TV station—WQED—said they wanted to do an educational show for children.

This was my chance to bring together all the things I loved: music, my imagination . . . and of course, entertainment for kids.

The night before the first episode of our show, which we called *The Children's Corner*, our station manager Dorothy Daniel gave every staff member a little gift.

It was a little tiger puppet.

I named him Daniel, after the person who gave him to me.

On our first episode, while trying to show a movie, the old film strip broke.

That was the first time I spoke through Daniel Tiger on air.
I never planned to use puppets on the show—I was just filling time.

One day, when our host Josie was having a bad day, she turned to the puppet and said...

I AM SO UPSET.

WELL, YOU JUST TELL ME ABOUT IT.

As she shared her feelings, something amazing happened.

REMEMBER, IT'S OKAY TO FEEL SAD SOMETIMES.

THANK YOU, DANIEL. I FEEL SO MUCH BETTER.

On the show, we started focusing on these puppet conversations, giving us a way to talk directly to kids like you.

It was like the make-believe conversations I used to have as a kid.

But now, *thousands* of kids were listening.

As I fan around backstage during each episode, my shoes kept squeaking.

SHHHH!

WHY'RE YOU CHANGING YOUR SHOES?

THESE ARE SNEAKERS WITH RUBBER SOLES. LESS SQUEAKY!

I FEEL LIKE THIS'LL BE IMPORTANT LATER.

In 1963, after I'd spent eight years doing puppets and playing music on *The Children's Corner*, a man named Dr. Fred Rainsberry asked if I would be the one on air.

I DON'T KNOW, I'M KINDA SHY.

DON'T WORRY. JUST LOOK INTO THE CAMERA...

AND PRETEND YOU'RE TALKING TO A CHILD.

At first, the show was called *Misterogers*. But eventually, we picked a better name...

Mister Rogers' Neighborhood.

Small town.

Clanging trolley.

CLING CLING

NEIGHBORHOOD TROLLEY

I filled it with so much of my life.

Kind neighbors.

MR. McFEELY, NAMED AFTER MY GRANDFATHER.

Music and make-believe.

LADY ELAINE, NAMED AFTER MY SISTER.

And of course . . .

I spoke to kids directly...
so they could understand that it's okay
to feel however they're feeling, even if
it's excited, sad, angry, or scared.

For 31 seasons and nearly 900 episodes, *Mister Rogers' Neighborhood* also taught kids to accept everyone, no matter their differences.

Back in the 1960s, when I heard that Black people weren't allowed to swim in the same pools as white people, I invited Officer Clemmons to come to mine.

Officer Clemmons was one of the first recurring Black characters on children's TV.

The actor, François, was surprised when I asked him to be a police officer on the show, but I told him that children need helpers, and I knew he'd be such a wonderful role model.

When President Nixon tried to cut funding for my TV channel, PBS, I went to Washington, DC, and spoke to Congress.

We asked for twenty million dollars to help grow national public television, but the senator in charge didn't seem to agree.

Then I told him what I do on my show...

In my life, I was shy and sad—and sometimes even mad.
Have you ever felt that way?
It's okay.
We all have moments when we feel blue.
But when we talk about our feelings, they become less upsetting and less scary.

Growing up, I used to think that being strong meant having big muscles.
But real strength comes from what is not seen.
Real strength comes from helping others.
When you do...

It's such a good feeling to know we're lifelong friends.
And as you grow older, I hope you'll be a helper.
You can help by sharing your kindness with
others and showing them love.
The greatest thing we can do is to let people
know that they are loved and capable of loving.

Thank you for spending this time with me.
You are a very special person.
There is only one you in the whole world.
There's never been anyone like you before,
and there never will be again.

I am Mister Rogers,
and I like you just the way you are.

"There are three ways to ultimate success: The first way is to be kind. The second way is to be kind. The third way is to be kind."

—FRED ROGERS

Timeline

MARCH 20, 1928	1951	JUNE 9, 1952	1954	1954	1955	1963
Born in Latrobe, PA	Begins first television job at NBC	Marries Joanne Byrd	Begins work as one of WQED's first employees in Pittsburgh, PA	*The Children's Corner* premieres	Enrolls part-time at Pittsburgh Theological Seminary	Becomes ordained minister

Talking with children
in Chicago, 1994

Mister Rogers with puppets
Henrietta Pussycat and X the Owl

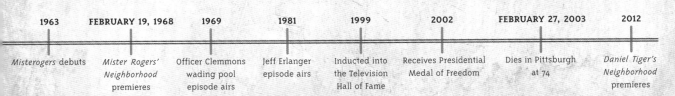

1963	FEBRUARY 19, 1968	1969	1981	1999	2002	FEBRUARY 27, 2003	2012
Misterogers debuts	*Mister Rogers' Neighborhood* premieres	Officer Clemmons wading pool episode airs	Jeff Erlanger episode airs	Inducted into the Television Hall of Fame	Receives Presidential Medal of Freedom	Dies in Pittsburgh at 74	*Daniel Tiger's Neighborhood* premieres

For Linda Simensky and Lesli Rotenberg,
for inviting us into the Neighborhood.
And in memory of Fred Rogers,
the kindest neighbor of all.
—B.M.

For Nick Lowe,
who embodies the spirit and values
Mister Rogers expressed
—Boop Boop (aka C.E.)

For historical accuracy, we used Mister Rogers's actual dialogue whenever possible. For more of Mister Rogers's true voice, we recommend and acknowledge the below titles. Special thanks to the extra kind Matthew Shiels and all our friends at Fred Rogers Productions and PBS for their input on early drafts.

SOURCES

Life's Journeys According to Mister Rogers by Fred Rogers (Hachette, 2005)

The World According to Mister Rogers by Fred Rogers (Hachette, 2003)

Dear Mister Rogers, Does It Ever Rain in Your Neighborhood?: Letters to Mister Rogers by Fred Rogers (Penguin, 1996)

The Last Interview: and Other Conversations by Fred Rogers, ed. with an introduction by David Bianculli (Melville House, 2021)

The Good Neighbor: The Life and Work of Fred Rogers by Maxwell King (Abrams, 2018)

Won't You Be My Neighbor? movie directed by Morgan Neville (2018)

"Can You Say . . . Hero?" by Tom Junod (*Esquire*, November 1998)

"Mister Rogers Changed My Life" by Angela C. Santomero (*New York Times*, September 21, 2012)

"When Fred Met Margaret: Mister Rogers' Mentor" by Sally Ann Flecker (University of Pittsburgh Medical School website, 2014)

"The Fred Rogers We Knew" by Soraya Roberts (*Hazlitt*, 2018)

"The Relics of Mister Rogers: 7 Emotional Items from the New Film *Won't You Be My Neighbor?*" by Anthony Breznican (*Entertainment Weekly*, June 9, 2018)

FURTHER READING FOR KIDS

Who Was Mister Rogers? by Diane Bailey (Penguin Workshop, 2019)

Fred's Big Feelings by Laura Renauld (Atheneum, 2020)

Hello, Neighbor! The Kind and Caring World of Mister Rogers by Matthew Cordell (Neal Porter Books, 2020)

ROCKY POND BOOKS • An imprint of Penguin Random House LLC, New York

First published in the United States of America by Rocky Pond Books, an imprint of Penguin Random House LLC, 2023

Text copyright © 2023 by Forty-four Steps, Inc. • Illustrations copyright © 2023 by Christopher Eliopoulos • Coloring by K.J. Díaz with Christopher Eliopoulos

Library of Congress Cataloging-in-Publication Data is available.

Photo on page 38: Fotos International/Courtesy of Getty Images; page 39 puppet photo by Bettmann/Courtesy of Getty Images;
photo with Chicago children courtesy of the Lynn Johnson Collection, Documentary Photography Archive, Mahn Center for Archives & Special Collections, Ohio University Libraries
Song lyrics by Fred M. Rogers, All Rights Reserved.

ISBN 9780593533307 • Manufactured in China • TOPL • 10 9 8 7 6 5 4 3 2 1

Designed by Jason Henry • Text set in Triplex • The artwork for this book was created digitally.